# AMISH ODYSSEY

Bottoms up

Windswept ...

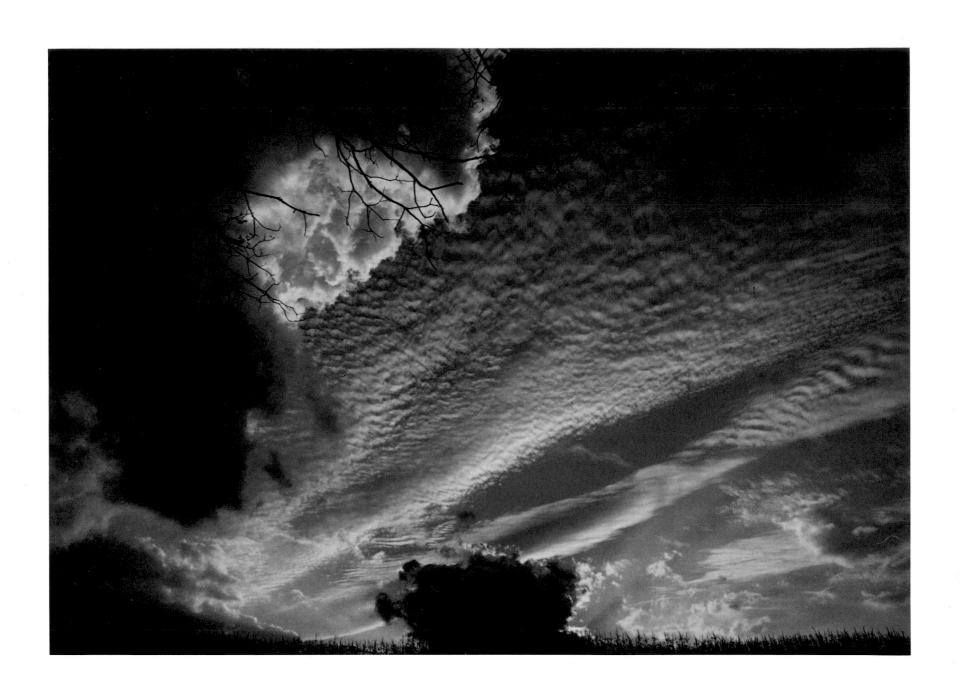

*almost Heaven*

Windswept II

almost home —

# Amish Odyssey

## PHOTOGRAPHS BY

## Bill Coleman

VAN DER MARCK EDITIONS · NEW YORK

*Editorial director:* Robert Walter

*Associate editor:* Jason Friedman

*Designer:* Jos.Trautwein/Bentwood Studio

All photographs © 1988 Bill Coleman

VAN DER MARCK EDITIONS
1133 Broadway, Suite 1301
New York, New York 10010

Separations by TH Graphics, Walnut, CA.
Printing and binding by Royal Smeets Offset BV, Netherlands.
First printing April 1988

**Library of Congress Cataloging-in-Publication Data**

Coleman, Bill, 1925-
  Amish odyssey.

  1. Amish——Pennsylvania——Pictorial works.
2. Pennsylvania—Social life and customs—Pictorial
works.  I. Title.
F160.M45C65  1988      974.8'0088287        87-40013
  ISBN 0-912383-49-6
  ISBN 0-912383-50-X (lim. ed.)

First printing May 1988

# INTRODUCTION

When Bill Coleman began to appear regularly in the remote Pennsylvania valley where all of the photographs in this book were taken, he was greeted with suspicion by its inhabitants, nearly all of whom are Old Order Amish. Unlike other more assimilated Amish—offspring of the strict religious group formed in sixteenth century Switzerland that emigrated to America in the eighteenth century—followers of the "Old Order" discourage intrusions from not only tourists but, indeed, any stranger. Since the valley is so remote and secluded that few people unknowingly stumble upon it, its seven hundred inhabitants have developed and maintain an almost self-contained and self-sufficient community.

As a result, although he respects private property and avoids showing his lens, Bill Coleman's presence on this tiny valley's roads and in its fields and woods has nonetheless been a source of conflict throughout his ten-year sojourn. Although for years no one saw Coleman's lens, initially he was threatening to them simply because he was a stranger    "an Englishman," an outsider with corrupting ideas that might lead their children astray. Parents counselled their children to "shun the stranger." When the Amish finally learned that Coleman was a photographer, they were little relieved; here was a man whose *metier* enabled him literally to steal their souls by pressing a single button.

As he gradually became known to the valley's residents, he was tolerated as a more or less benign presence and acknowledged for who he was: a photographer trying to document their daily lives without exploiting them. When Coleman first decided to sell some of his photographs, he established a trust fund, administered by an elder of the community, to provide the valley's residents with medical care. He continues to fund the trust on a regular basis with a portion of any income he earns from the photographs.

As the Amish came to know Coleman as a person, he came to know them as distinctive individuals. Over the years certain people—especially children—have reappeared in his photographs. A boy named Ezra and his sisters, for example, are the subjects of a number of the photographs in this book. He has come to respect the adults and to cherish the children. He relishes talking with children and regularly brings them acceptable presents—ice skates, dolls, and such.

His familiarity with his subjects accounts in part for the strength of his images. Through the powerful way he captures individual personalities, he creates wholly original compositions from subject matter that might easily have been rendered sentimental and hackneyed. These are not merely photographs of the Amish lifestyle; they are also portraits of memorable individuals engaged in various real-life activities who happen to be members of a small Amish sect.

Although the Amish might tolerate his presence, Coleman knows they will never welcome him. He realizes that he must use his telephoto lens and often conceal himself, or his camera, if his subjects are neither to take offense nor simply to walk—or run—away. And

through it all, he continually and repeatedly asks himself why he takes these photographs, testing and retesting his convictions and motivations, until he is, as he puts it, "torn up inside."

He has given his subjects photographs, most of which they find pleasing. They will usually accept the pictures, but only in exchange for something else. When they refuse for religious reasons to accept them, it is always with some reluctance.

Bill Coleman has heard admonishments ranging from gentle suggestion to pointed reproach, all of which reinforce his perhaps inevitable anxiety about intruding into his subjects' lives. Moments after he took a particular photograph of an older couple riding past in their buggy, they stopped, and the woman leaned out and said, "You have stolen my soul." The hurt and guilt remained with him for a long time. Some time later, when he related the incident to a writer who collects his work, he was told, "On the contrary; you are preserving her soul." Although he felt temporarily better, he remained troubled until he later had the opportunity to show the couple that their faces did not appear in the shot. And then, when they told him they liked the photograph, he was finally relieved.

Why, then, does Coleman continue his photographic excursions into this valley? Over the course of his ten-year odyssey, he has had ample time to riddle the complexity of reasons.

There are issues of scholarship. He feels a responsibility to document the way of life in the tiny community before it disappears, an event he considers all but inevitable. After a decade's observation, he remains amazed at the people's ability to maintain traditional values and a self-sufficient lifestyle entirely at odds with ultra-technological twentieth century America. And although he knows that his contribution to our understanding of the Amish way of life is not an exhaustive survey—more a collection of impressions, small insights—Coleman also realizes that in his absence the customs and traditions of these people could disappear and remain unknown.

Then there are the personal reasons. "When I'm in the valley I feel like I've shed a couple of layers of plastic that are usually all around me," he said. His photographs are loving and even envious. Talking about a favored photographic location, Threepenny Lane, he quips, "I've often wished that was my address." Taking these particular photographs has truly become an obsession. He gave up a successful portrait studio to devote himself full-time to taking photographs in this valley.

*Amish Odyssey*—an amble in images and words through one of America's most traditional Amish communities—captures the spirit of an extraordinary group of people. Comments throughout are the photographer's, juxtaposed with the pictures whenever an image reminds Coleman of a significant incident, entertaining story, or provocative detail. As a result, *Amish Odyssey* can be read as a sort of journal, the record of Bill Coleman's journey into the very heart of a small Amish clan.

*morning ritual*

We get this fog in the spring and the fall. Because of the valley's configuration the
fog just stays put until ten or ten thirty in the morning. The beauty of this is that I can
hear a buggy or children or most anything from a goodly distance — long before they
see me. And if my luck holds, I might make an image of them as they approach me
and again, seconds later, as they pass.

morning ritual II

Paradise found —

I had hoped that the fog and the distance had kept me relatively anonymous. In fact I was certain of it. Yet when the buggy passed, a woman leaned out and said, very clearly, "You have stolen my soul." The hurt stayed with me a long time. Though I've heard it a few times since from others, it is that woman in the fog who stays in my memory.

Roughing it . . .

When you get to the valley you immediately recognize that something is radically differ-
ent. It starts with the lay of the land. It's manicured exquisitely. Maybe it's the lack of
telephone poles or electric lines, but there's more to it than that. There isn't a piece, a
square foot, of ground that's wasted, nor are there weeds. There's a cleanliness, an
order. There's a harmony between what they're doing for the land and whatever they're
doing in their lives.

*Ladies in Waiting*

Clusters

*To an evening sing —*

*During the summer, teenagers attend a Sunday evening "sing" and perhaps take part in a bit of socializing. At times you can hear the gentle murmur of these warm folk songs from half a mile away.*

*Rural Delivery II*

*First one home...*

When I'm in the valley I try to spend time talking with Amish kids because you can learn an awful lot from kids. There's such openness and honesty; they've been having a love affair all their lives with the earth and day-to-day living. Living — I have to emphasize that. They're faced with that thing, with life. I sense in their faces a purity that comes from not having been stultified, or call it what you will, from all the things our kids are exposed to.

Little Women

Almost Late

Brothers four —

Little mothers

This reminds me of seventeenth century Dutch paintings in which you might see a woman suppressing a laugh with her hand. This must be one of the last places in America where this old European trait can be seen.

Ball game?

To me, there's a world of beauty and mystery to be found in groups of children. You never know what they're going to be doing, so there are compositional things, there are facial things, there are all kinds of things that you must be prepared for. At the same time you must make sure that you're doing it in a most unobtrusive manner.

all sizes — all shapes...

Someday...

Buddies...

One Days Work IV

Belgians Four

First love

Pair of jacks

*Soon I saw why he was just standing there. What amazed me was his unflappable stance in the presence of these half-ton behemoths. He never moved a muscle as he stood there to guide the cows from one field to another. It was as if he'd been doing this all his life — and he probably had.*

From little acorns

*He seemed lost. A few moments later he turned…*     50

*Innocence*

...and I saw this face of exquisite innocence surrounded by a straw halo. Surely an angel on earth.

Sez Who?

*of bread and bonnets...*

Lunch Recess...

Ezra's Sisters

*Round up*

The boy with the hat is rounding up his sisters to come in for lunch. Some of the sisters are older, some are younger; he has no brothers. He knows his responsibilities. He's a very special boy. He's fun-loving, and whenever he sees me he laughs and laughs and laughs.

First Date

The Vanilla hat

Two on three Penny Lane

*On Schoolhouse Lane*

*I think my own sense of who and what the Amish are is a visceral, emotional thing. I have not become a scholar of the Amish or read an excessive number of books on the subject. I would rather find out about them by small, little surprises, little cameos here and there that constantly happen.*

One more turn.

Last stand

Last Load II

Dangling family...

*Thursday's Wedding III*

Weddings are held usually in October and usually on the last two Thursdays. That's because the end of October is the only time of the year when they can stop and relax somewhat and still enjoy the wonderful weather outdoors.

Sundays best

*September morning*

Ad Infinitum

Once upon a sky

For years this schoolhouse has been a favorite subject of mine but usually when children are cavorting
around it, as it appears in the following few pages.
The children become wonderfully animated stick
figures against the backdrop of the snow.

I went out one day, however, when there was no
one around, no activity, and it turned me off a little
bit. Plus the sky wasn't quite right. As I was getting
ready to put my cameras away I saw the unex-
pected — true serendipity. The rays burst out just,
just right. It was a theatrical performance just for
me, and I almost applauded. I took the picture (left).

Last one out ...

Show off —

the Kick...

Ice Frolics...

93

*Rural Frisbees*

When this bunch of boys began throwing their hats up in the air, I couldn't believe what I was seeing. Maybe it was the bell announcing the end of ice-skating recess — or maybe they saw me. Whatever, it was too good not to record. I started, and went through three rolls of film. I got back, had the film processed, and only one out of maybe ninety photographs came out halfway decently. Almost every one of them was blurred, and it dawned on me why. I was so excited when I was shooting that I didn't realize that I was shaking the camera.

I got to know an Amish teacher rather well. She was maybe sixty, or so. She had a grandmotherly approach to the children. One day during recess I said to her, "I have never ever heard these children raise their voices, at any hour of school. In our schools you can hear the kids from a mile away. Why not here? They're playing games, but they're quiet." She said, "Well, did you ever hear an Amish adult raise his voice?"

*Relief ahead*

*Sometimes I wonder why this simple house so often captures my attention. I expect this affair will continue for some time.*

White wash

When I go out to the valley, I go out with great joy, and yet at the same time I expect
to be humbled again by seeing something I never saw before. I could be looking at a
place from the same point of view as always, standing at the exact same point, and I
will see something I've never seen. And when I do, all of a sudden, it's great joy, but
at the same time I feel, Idiot, why didn't you see it before? It was here, you know.

White Velvet

*I was getting ready to photograph these milk cans. It was early April, and there was no snow, but it was cold, gray, and a bit ominous. Suddenly a blizzard coated everything white with snow, and I got this exposure. But there was no time for a second one. The snow immediately melted — thanks to the warm milk.*

Connie's other fence...

He was on his way out. I saw what a lovely photograph the dog running before the horse would make, so I took the picture (above). I was getting ready to put the camera down when I saw the man make a wide circle and head back in the direction he had come from at full speed. I made this shot of him returning to his house. I waited, and a few minutes later he headed out to the woods again. I saw why he had returned home. He had gone out hunting, and he had forgotten his gun.

Nina's choice . . .

Hitching...

"Piece of cake"...

*You don't make assumptions about the Amish, even if you know them. In this remote valley one dichotomy begets another. Because of various Biblical interpretations and traditions there are many varied groups of generically Old Order Amish in this one valley. I have noticed obvious variations in the color of buggy tops, the design and color of clothing, the way suspenders are worn, and so on. But these are only the obvious variations. I know that the more subtle differences are philosophical. These deeply held beliefs determine how much deviation from tradition can be allowed for the sake of economic well-being. This ancient gasoline engine, for example, is what one farmer uses to get grain to the top of his silo. He has since covered it with a tarpaulin. But this is how I see it in my mind's eye— iced with snow, truly a piece of cake.*

Respite II

One last run

Tracks

*For generations past and those to come, this solemn processional will be part of their*
*life as well as the final journey. When I witnessed this scene—the buggies following*
*the wagon bearing a plain coffin—the simple dignity and reverential silence were*
*overwhelming. It was a requiem unto itself.*

*Processional*

133

Hostetlers farm

Solemn Return

Over the years I've made countless photographs of this one cemetery. There are others in the valley, but this single acre perched high on a hill has a character and ambiance that defy my efforts to describe it. These simple headstones, often bearing names crudely scratched in by hand, seem most fitting markers for lives dedicated to the basics.

Faces...

Infant...

*of things to come*

This is typical of what I've seen so often. They are coming down a snow-covered road toward me on their way back from school. They see me. He's probably around seven or eight. She's maybe five or six. Only when they see me does he instinctively, or intuitively, reach for her hand, and hand-in-hand they go past me. Probably won't say a word. If I do, they might smile a moment and keep on walking. After a goodly distance — almost always six or seven hundred feet — he turns his head back and looks at me. When he sees that I'm not pursuing them, that I'm minding my own business, only then does he release her hand. And then they dance their way on.

Sunday's Silo.

# DEDICATION

*Dedicated to my friend Bill Timmerman,*

*who taught me to see.*

## ACKNOWLEDGMENTS

Deeply felt thanks to Kathy Davies, Carl Inglesby,
and Jan Richardson, all of whom made slight
of my many shortcomings.

I thank Joe Trautwein for his imaginative layout.

And above all, I thank the Old Order Amish of this
unnamed valley who, for ten years, have stoically tolerated
my incursions and occasional transgressions.

Perhaps this book will explain to them my love for their very special valley...
but I nurture no illusions.